the **REALLY** funny

joke book for kids

Mickey MacIntyre

The Really Funny LOL! Joke Book For Kids. Over 200 Side-Splitting, Rib-Tickling Jokes: Guaranteed To Make You LAUGH OUT LOUD!

Mickey MacIntyre

ISBN 978-1-909855-40-3

Contents

the **REALLY** funny....

4

Top Ten Tips For Telling Jokes

Practice, Practice, Practice!

Know your joke. Ok so it's only a short joke, but mess it up and no one will be laughing. Make sure you know your joke 'off by heart' and practice it in front of a mirror. Learning your lines means you can concentrate on 'telling' the joke instead of just reading it.

Know when to be quiet!

Don't start explaining the joke the second you have told it. Let your audience work it out for a few seconds and they will laugh when they 'get' it.

Don't tell jokes that could get you in trouble. Avoid subjects that might fall into this category like rude or insensitive jokes. All the jokes in The REALLY Funny Doctor! Doctor! Joke Book are clean and trouble free!

Don't announce you are about to tell a joke.
Your audience is more likely to find a joke funny if they don't have a big announcement that they are about to hear something 'REALLY FUNNY'.

Don't tell everyone how funny your joke is before you tell it.
It makes your audience expect too much.

Don't laugh at your own jokes until your audience has laughed.
Give your audience time to 'get' the joke. Most of the best joke tellers tell their jokes

the REALLY funny....

with a 'straight' face.

Choose your moment.

There are bad times to tell a joke. For example if someone is really busy, sick, sad or has hurt themselves. Pick a time when everyone is in a good mood and wants to have some fun.

Take your time. Don't rush. Speeding through words too quickly will make it difficult to understand and if you have to repeat a joke, it's not as funny.

Speak clearly and make sure you 'get' the joke before you tell it. Think about the way the punch line should sound and practice it. If you think it's funny someone else will too!

Study your favourite comedians or anyone else you see on TV or youtube.

Watch how they 'work' the audience, how they deliver their punchlines, what they do with their hands. Learn from the professionals!

Enjoy!

the **REALLY** funny....

Now For The REALLY Funny LOL! Jokes........

Teacher: Whoever answers my next question, can go home.
One boy throws his bag out the window.
Teacher: Who just threw that?
Boy: Me! I'm going home now!

Why do bicycles fall over?
Because they are two-tired!

What did one raindrop say to the other raindrop?
My plop is bigger than your plop!

What does a bankrupt frog say?
Baroke, baroke, baroke!

How are eyes and schools similar?
They both have pupils!

What is the funniest soda?
Joke-a-cola!

What do cats call mice on
skateboards?
Meals on Wheels!

Doctor to a rich man: Do you prefer
a local anesthesia?
Rich man: I would prefer an
imported one!

Why can't skeletons play church music?
Because they have no organs!

How can you get four suits for £1?
Buy a deck of cards!

Pupil: Will you punish me for something that I didn't do?
Teacher: No of course not.
Pupil: That's good because I didn't do my homework!

What is a computer virus?
A terminal illness!

the **REALLY** funny....

Why couldn't the
cat use a computer?
Because he kept attacking the
mouse!

Why did the teacher write the lesson
on the windows?
He wanted the lesson to be very
clear!

Why did the turtle
cross the road?
To get to the Shell
station!

What do elves learn in school?
The Elf-abet!

 What's the funniest
motorbike in the world?
A yamahahahahahahahahahahaha!

What do you get when you put 10
ducks in a box?
A box of quackers!

What do you get if you cross an
elephant with a fish?
Swimming Trunks!

What were Tarzans last words?
Who greased the vine?!

What kind of eggs does a wicked chicken lay?
Deviled eggs!

How does a farmer count a herd of cows?
With a Cowculator!

Why couldn't the cat watch a movie on the DVD player?
He kept hitting the PAWS button!

Why do dogs scratch themselves?
Because they are the ones who know where it itches!

What did the frog order at
McDonald's?
French flies and a diet croak!

What do you call a fossil
that doesn't ever want to
work?
Lazy bones!

What kinds of birds are good at
writing?
Pen-guins!

Which nut has no shell?
A doughnut!

the REALLY funny....

Why was the maths 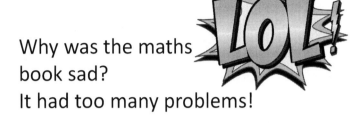 book sad?
It had too many problems!

Did you hear about the dog that went to a flea circus?
No, what happened?
He stole the show!

How do you apologise to a parrot?
With an a-POLLY-gy!

What do you call a dinosaur with an extensive vocabulary?
A thesaurus!

 How deep can a frog go?
Knee-deep Knee-deep!

What did the mayonnaise say to the refrigerator?
Close the door, I'm dressing!

How can you tell if you have a stupid dog?
It chases parked cars!

How do you make one disappear?
Add a 'g' or an 'n' to 'one'!

Mother: Are you talking back to me?!"

Son: Erm yes! That's kind of how communication works!

Which keys are too big to carry in your pocket?
A donkey, a turkey and a monkey!

What is a frog's favorite game?
Croaket!

What did the mother ghost tell the baby ghost when he ate too fast?
Stop goblin your food!

What is the strongest animal?
A snail because he carries his house
on his back!

What is a monkey's favorite
Christmas carol?
Jungle Bells!

What did one mountain say to
the other mountain after the
earthquake?
It's not my fault!

Why is a swordfish's nose 11 inches
long?
If it were 12 inches long it would be
a foot!

the REALLY funny....

Why are tennis games so loud?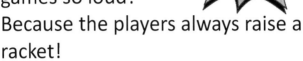
Because the players always raise a racket!

What does a brain do when it sees a friend across the street?
It gives a brain wave!

What is Dracula's favorite sport?
Bat-minton!

What's it like to be kissed by a vampire?
It's a pain in the neck!

 I taught my dog not to beg at the table.

How did you do that?

I let him taste my mum's cooking. He didn't want to beg any more after that!

Why is it so cold at Christmas?
Because it's in Decembrrrrr!

Who is the most famous shark writer?
William Sharkspeare!

Who is your best friend at school?
Your princi-pal!

Who was the greatest financier in the Bible?
Noah. He was floating his stock while everyone else was in liquidation!

Roses are red
Violets are blue
Your face looks funny
Lets all laugh at you!

Why was the computer cold?
It left its Windows open!

Do engines have ears?
Yes, engineers!

What did the lawyer name his
daughter?
Sue!

Which streets do ghosts haunt?
Dead ends!

Why are frogs so happy?
They eat whatever bugs them!

Which state do pencils come from?
Pencil-vania!

Why do birds fly south in the
winter?
Because it's too far to walk!

the REALLY funny....

A little girl had just
finished her first
week of school.
I'm just wasting my time,' she said to
her mother.
I can't read, I can't write, and they
won't let me talk!

If you had five sweets on your desk
and the boy next to you took two,
what would you get?
A fight!

What is the difference between a
doctor and a lawyer?
A doctor rides in the ambulance. A
lawyer rides outside, chasing it!

What do you call a flying ear?

Earplane!

What did the
hamburger name its baby?
Patty!

What's the strongest vegetable?
A muscle sprout!

Why is it hard to play cards in the jungle?
There are too many cheetahs!

the REALLY funny....

What do ghosts drink at breakfast?
Coffee with scream and sugar!

Where can you get milkshakes?
From scared cows!
What do you call a bear with no teeth?
A gummy bear!

What is the difference between an outlaw and an in-law?
Outlaws are wanted!

What happens when two snails have a fight?
They slug it out!

What did the hurricane say to the other hurricane?
I have my eye on you!

What do you get when you cross a cow and a duck?
Milk and quackers!

What do Eskimos get from sitting on the ice too long?
Pola-roids!

Teacher: Who can tell me what an atom is?
Pupil: The man who went out with Eve!

the REALLY funny....

Dad, can you write  in the dark?

I think so. What do you want me to write?

Your name on this school report card!

Who is the most famous ghost detective?

Sherlock Bones!

Why were the early days of history called the dark ages?

Because there were so many knights!

How do you make a tissue dance?

Put a little boogie in it!

 What school subject is a witch good at?
Spelling!

What does a cloud wear under his raincoat?
Thunderwear!

What is an astronaut's favorite place on a computer?
The Space bar!

What's a snake's favorite school subject?
Hissssstory!

What did the hungry computer eat?
Chips, one byte at a time!

How does the man in the moon
eat his food?
In satellite dishes!

What do you call sweet corn that
joins the army?
Kernel!

Where was the Queen crowned?
On her head!

Why did the tomato turn red?
Because it saw the salad dressing!

What did one star say to the other star when they met?
Glad to meteor!

What did the big chimney say to the little chimney?
You are too young to smoke!

What kind of cats like to go bowling?
Alley cats!

Why was there a bug in the computer?
Because it was looking for a byte to eat!

the REALLY funny....

How much money do you have when you combine touch, vision, smell, hearing and taste?
Five cents (sense)!

Why do gorillas have big nostrils?
They have big fingers!

What do ghosts eat at Halloween?
Boo-berry pie!

What do you get when you cross a potato with an onion?
A potato with watery eyes!

 **Teacher:** Here is a maths problem. If your dad earned £300 a week and he gave your mum 75%, what would he have?
Pupil: A heart attack!

Dad: I thought you were supposed to wash the dishes after you do your homework! Why are you watching TV?
Son: I haven't done my homework yet!

What did the dog say when he sat on the sandpaper?
Rough! Rough!

What did the calculator say to the other calculator?
You can count on me!

What did the student say to the math worksheet?
I'm not a therapist, solve your own problems!

What happens when it rains cats and dogs?
You have to be careful not to step on a poodle!

Why do fish live in salt water?
Because pepper makes them sneeze!

What do you call a famous fish?
A Starfish!

What did the right hemisphere say to the left hemisphere when they could not agree on anything?
Let's split!

Which president came after the first President of the USA?
The second one!

What is the longest word in the dictionary?
The word 'smiles' because there is a mile between each 's'!

the REALLY funny....

Why did the
computer squeak?
Because someone stepped on its
mouse!

What do you call an old snowman?
Water!

How do you stop yourself getting a
summer cold?
Catch it in the winter!

How do you like going to school?
The going bit is fine, and I don't mind
the coming home bit too, but I'm not
too keen on the bit in-between!

Teacher: Why are you late?"

Pupil: Because of a sign down the road.

Teacher: What do the sign have to do with you being late?

Pupil: The sign said, 'School Ahead, Go Slow!

Why did the fastest cat in school get suspended?

'Coz he was a cheetah!

How did the teacher knit a suit of armor?

She used steel wool!

the REALLY funny....

How do you like going to school?
The going bit is fine, and I don't mind the coming home bit too, but I'm not too keen on the bit in-between!

What did the one tornado say to the other?
Let's twist again like we did last summer!

What is the laziest mountain in the whole world?
Mount Ever-rest!

What did you learn in school today?
Not enough, I have to go back tomorrow!

What did they award the man that invented the door knocker?
The No-bell Prize!

What do you call a cat that is frozen?
Catsicle!

What's the different between a cat and a comma?
A cat has claws at the end of paws; a comma is a pause at the end of a clause!

Were you long in the hospital?
No, I was the same size that I am now!

the REALLY funny....

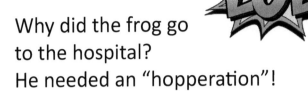

Why did the frog go
to the hospital?
He needed an "hopperation"!

Where do little ghosts learn to shout
"BOO!" so loudly?
In noisery school!

Why did the student drown?
All her grades were below C
(sea) -level!

What did the lightning bolt say to
the other lightning bolt?
You're shocking!

 What happened
to the frog's car
when his parking meter expired?
It got toad!

What does one eye say to the other
eye?
Just between the two of us,
something smells!

What kind of vegetable is jealous?
A green bean!

Why are cooks mean?
Because they beat up eggs and whip
the cream!

42

Why do fish avoid the computer?
So they don't get caught in the
Internet!

What did the boy octopus say to the
girl octopus?
I want to hold your hand, hand,
hand, hand, hand, hand, hand, hand!

Why do dogs bury bones in the
ground?
Because you can't bury them in
trees!

Why are black cats such good
singers?
They're very mew-sical!

Customer: Waiter, there's a fly swimming in my soup.
Waiter: So what do you want me to do, call a lifeguard?!

Teacher: What is the outside of a tree called?
Pupil: I don't know.
Teacher: Bark, boy, bark.
Pupil: no. I'm not a dog!

What is a math teacher's favorite dessert?
Pi!

What type of
lightning likes to play sports?
Ball lightning!

Why did the sheep say "moo"?
It was learning a new language!

What happens when
two frogs collide?
They got tongue
tied!

What's the worst thing about being
an octopus?
Having to wash your hands before
eating!

How do you make a goldfish old?

Lose the 'g'!

What do you get when you cross a computer with an elephant?
Lots of memory!

Why is football such a messy sport?
Because of all the dribbling!

Why is it good to have a snake for a librarian?
Because they tell everyone to "Sssssssshhh!"

What did the lettuce say to the celery?
Stop stalking me!

How did the boy feel after being caned?
Absolutely whacked!

Why are sponges and brains similar?
They both like to soak things up.

What do you say when you meet a two headed monster?
Hello. Hello!

Which object is king of the classroom?
The ruler!

Would you like some Egyptian Pie?
What's Egyptian pie?
You know, the kind mummy used to make!

What is a dolphin's favorite TV show?
Whale of Fortune!

Teacher: George, how can you prove the earth is round?
Pupil: I never said it was!

the REALLY funny....

How do you know
Santa Claus is good at karate?
He has a black belt!

What do you get when you cross a
computer and a life-guard?
A screensaver!

What do you call a pony with a sore
throat?
A little horse!

What do seven day of dieting do?
They make one weak!

 What do you get when you cross a thought with a light bulb?
A bright idea!

What do you get when you cross a teacher and a vampire?
Lots of blood tests!

Mother: What was the first thing you learned in class?
Daughter: How to talk without moving my lips!

How do you wake up a sleeping Lady Gaga?
You pok-er face!

What does it mean when the barometer is falling? It means whoever nailed it up didn't do a good job!

What did one flag say to the other flag?
Nothing, it's just waved!

Teacher: What's 2 and 2?
Pupil: 4
Teacher: That's good.
Pupil: Good? That's perfect!

Where do all the cool mice live?
In their mousepads!

Why did the computer keep
sneezing?
It had a virus!

Why did the teacher wear
sunglasses?
Because her students were bright!

What do you call it when it rains
chickens and ducks?
Fowl weather!

What did the spider do on the
computer?
Made a website!

What do fashion
conscious frogs wear?
A Jumpsuit!

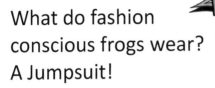

Which country do sweets come
from?
Sweeten!

Teacher: Where is your homework?
Pupil: Some aliens from outer space
borrowed it so they could study how
the human brain works!

What do vegetables wish for, more
than anything else in the whole
world?
Peas (peace) on earth!

 What do
Snowmen have for
Breakfast?
Snowflakes!

What did one toe say to the other?
Don't look now, but there's a heel
following us!

Why was the zombie so grumpy?
She woke up too early in the
mourning.

Did you hear about the wooden car
with the wooden wheels and the
wooden engine?
It wooden go!

What do you call a cheese that's not yours?
Nacho Cheese!

What did the ground say to the earthquake?
You crack me up!

What do you take before every meal?
A seat!

What's the best thing to give your parents for Christmas?
A list of everything you want!

Which sharks would you find at a
construction site?
Hammerhead sharks!

What did the duck say when he
bought
lipstick?
Put it on my bill!

Where does a rabbit go when it loses
its tail?
To the re-tail shop, of course!

How do you catch a rabbit?
Hide behind a tree and make carrot
noises!

What do you get
when a male chicken and a male cow
start an argument?
A cock and bull story!

If a long dress is evening wear, what
is a suit of armor?
Silverware!

What do skeletons always order at a
restaurant?
Spare ribs!

What do you call a fly with no wings?
A walk!

Why was 6 afraid of 7?

Because 7 8 9!

How does a frog feel when he has a broken leg?
Unhoppy!

What do vampires have at eleven o'clock every day?
A coffin break!

What do a magician and a footballer have in common?
Both of them can do hat tricks!

the REALLY funny....

Where do fortune tellers dance?
At the crystal ball!

Why do turkeys always go "gobble, gobble" at meal times?
Because they never learned good table manners!

What do you call a fake stone in Ireland?
A Sham-rock!

How do you catch a squirrel?
Climb into a tree and act like a nut!

What kind of bow can't be tied?
A rainbow!

Teacher: Tell me something about oysters, Johnny.
Pupil: They are very lazy. They are always in beds.

Where did Ivy go to become famous?
Holly-Wood!

Why do plants hate maths?
Because it gives them square roots!

How do you cut a wave?
With a sea saw!

the REALLY funny....

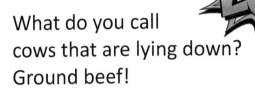

What do you call cows that are lying down?
Ground beef!

What did the turtle wear to keep warm?
A turtle neck!

What is the world's biggest ant?
An Eleph-ant!

What happens if you see twin witches?
You won't be able to see which witch is witch!

 What do you get when you cross an apple and a Christmas tree?
A pineapple!

What did one clever penny say to the other clever penny?
If we get together, we could make some cents (sense)!

What is big, red and prickly, has three eyes and eats rocks?
A big, red, prickly three eyed rock eater!

How do hurricanes see?
With their eye!

What do you get when you cross poison ivy with a 4-leaf clover?
A rash of good luck

Why did the boy eat his maths homework?
Because the teacher told him it was a piece of cake!

What do prisoners use to call each other?
Cell phones!

What can a whole orange do that half an orange can never do?
Look round!

Teacher: Why are you doing your maths multiplication on the floor?
Pupil: You told me to do it without using tables!

What did one magnet say to the other?
I find you very attractive!

Why was Cinderella thrown off the team?
Because she ran away from the ball!

What do you get from a pampered cow?
Spoilt milk!

the **REALLY** funny....

What flower do you wear on your face?
Two-lips!

What did the elevator say to the other elevator?
I think I'm coming down with something!

Teacher: You aren't paying attention. Are you having trouble hearing?
Pupil: No, teacher I'm having trouble listening!

What do you call a swarm of monster bees?
Zombees!

What do you call a fake noodle?
An impasta!

What always ends everything?
The letter 'G'!

More REALLY Funny Joke Books

You may also enjoy
**'The REALLY Funny
Knock! Knock! Joke
Book For Kids'.**

And

**'The REALLY Funny
Doctor! Doctor! Joke
Book For Kids'.**

Plus look out for more *REALLY* **Funny**
joke books from **Mickey MacIntyre**
coming soon. Just search Mickey
MacIntyre on **Amazon**.

LOL! Joke Book For Kids

37953417R10039

Printed in Great Britain
by Amazon